REPTILES
AND
AMPHIBIANS
DICTIONARY

An A to Z of cold-blooded creatures

D1122891

Author Clint Twist
Editorial Manager Ruth Hooper
Editorial Assistant Emily Hawkins
Art Director Ali Scrivens
Designer Julia Harris
Production Clive Sparling
Consultant Zoologist Valerie Davies
Illustrators Barry Croucher (Wildlife Art Ltd), Sandra Doyle (Wildlife Art Ltd), Ian Jackson (Wildlife Art Ltd), Mike Rowe (Wildlife Art Ltd), Myke Taylor (Wildlife Art Ltd), Gill Tomblin

Created and produced by
Andromeda Children's Books
An imprint of Pinwheel Ltd
Winchester House
259-269 Old Marylebone Road
London
NW1 5XJ
UK
www.pinwheel.co.uk

This edition produced in 2005 for Scholastic Inc.
Published by Tangerine Press, an imprint of Scholastic Inc.
557 Broadway, New York, NY 10012

Scholastic and Tangerine Press and associated logos are trademarks of Scholastic Inc.

Copyright © 2005 Andromeda Children's Books

ISBN 0-439-80693-3

Printed in China

Information Icons

Throughout this dictionary there are special icons next to each entry. These give you more information about each creature.

Globes

These show you where each animal can be found in the world. Small red dots clearly show the locations.

Size Comparison Pictures

Next to each entry you will see a symbol, either a hand or a man, next to a red icon of each animal listed. The hand or man shows you the size of each animal in real life.

7 inches

The first symbol is a human adult's hand, which measures about 7 inches (18 cm) from the wrist to the tip of the longest finger. Some animals are smaller than this, so the size comparison shows you its size.

6 feet

The second symbol is an adult human. With its arms outstretched, the armspan measures about 6 feet (1.8 m). This symbol shows the size of really big animals.

REPTILES AND AMPHIBIANS
DICTIONARY

An A to Z of cold-blooded creatures

tangerine Press®

an imprint of

■SCHOLASTIC

www.scholastic.com

Cold-blooded Life

Red-eyed
tree frog

Reptiles and amphibians are part of the animal kingdom known as vertebrates (animals with backbones). All reptiles and amphibians are cold-blooded—their bodies do not produce heat so they rely on the environment for warmth. Mammals and birds are warm-blooded, and their bodies produce heat. There are about 8,000 reptile species, and about 5,000 species of amphibians.

Amphibians

An amphibian's body is covered with skin that is rough and "warty," or smooth and slimy. Amphibians lay soft, jelly-covered eggs. When the eggs hatch, the young begin a juvenile stage, which later develops into an adult stage.

Some amphibians spend their whole lives in water, but most spend some time on land when they are adults. Amphibians are divided into two main groups: frogs and toads; and newts and salamanders. Another group is the worm-like caecilians.

Eastern newt

Reptiles

Reptiles have skin that is protected by tough scales. They are completely adapted to life on land. Most reptiles lay eggs but some lizards and snakes give birth to live young.

Emerald tree
skink

The reptile groups are: tortoises and turtles; lizards; snakes; amphisbaenians; tuatara; and crocodiles and alligators. Most reptiles live on land but some, such as sea turtles, live their entire lives in water. They do return to land to lay their eggs.

Yellow-blotched map turtle

Habitats

Being cold-blooded means that reptiles and amphibians rely on the sun and surroundings to keep their bodies warm. They are most numerous in hot climates. In colder climates, they often hibernate to escape the winter cold. Amphibians spend part of their lives in water, and most return to water in order to lay eggs. They don't go too far from ponds or rivers. Reptiles do well in hot, dry climates. There are many different desert lizards and tortoises.

Black mamba

5

Crocodiles and alligators

Crocodiles and alligators are large reptiles with long bodies and four short legs. They live near water and are excellent swimmers. The skin of crocodiles and alligators is covered with hard, bony plates called scutes. These reptiles are meat-eaters and often hunt for prey on land as well as in the water.

Nile crocodile

Turtles and tortoises

Turtles and tortoises are four-legged reptiles with a domed carapace, or shell, protecting their bodies. The carapace is usually made of hard plates fused together into a rigid shell. Tortoises live on land, while most turtles live in or near water. Freshwater turtles spend long periods out of the water, sunning themselves. Sea turtles, such as the hawskbill, live their entire lives swimming in the ocean.

Red-eared turtle

Lizards

Lizards are a big group of reptiles, ranging from very small to the very large Komodo dragon. Most lizards have four legs but some species have only two back legs, or no legs at all. Lizard skin is covered with scales. These are usually small and round, but some lizards have big, spiny scutes that are more like a crocodile's.

Granite night lizard

Snakes

Snakes are legless, mostly meat-eating reptiles. They vary in length from 4 inches (10 cm) to 33 feet (10 m), and are covered with small scales. Snakes are found in most habitats. Some snakes, such as boas and pythons, kill by constriction—they squeeze their victim so it cannot breathe. Other snakes inject venom with sharp fangs. Some snakes' venom is strong enough to kill an adult human.

Red spitting cobra

Frogs and toads

Frogs and toads are amphibians with large eyes, no tail, and powerful back legs. The eggs hatch in water to become tadpoles, which undergo a metamorphosis into the adult form. A difference between frogs and toads is that toads usually have bumpy skin but a frog's skin is smooth. Toads also tend to be slower-moving. In tropical regions, many frogs live in trees.

Fire-bellied toad

Slimy salamander

Newts and salamanders

Newts and salamanders are amphibians that usually have four legs and a long tail, but some have only two front legs. Some salamanders spend their entire lives in water, while others live on land as adults. Newts tend to be smaller than salamanders. Some newts live in water all the time, others only when breeding.

Aa

Max length: 9½ inches (24 cm)
Reptile

Ajolote

The ajolote, also known as the mole lizard, is one of the world's strangest reptiles. It belongs to the group known as amphisbaenians or "worm lizards." The ajolote is found in the Baja peninsula in Mexico. It has a long, snakelike body, with a tiny pair of short, powerful legs just behind its head. It has clawed feet, which it uses for burrowing underground.

Max length: 5 feet (1.5 m)
Reptile

Aldabra Island tortoise

The Aldabra Island tortoise is found on just one tropical island in the Indian Ocean. It grows to rival the Galápagos tortoise in size, with a carapace (shell) up to 5 feet (1.5 m) long, and can weigh up to 600 lbs. (272 kg). The Aldabra Island tortoise is endangered and protected. A small number have been introduced on nearby islands.

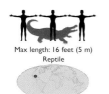

Max length: 16 feet (5 m)
Reptile

Alligator (American)

The American alligator can grow up to 16 feet (5 m) in length. It is found in lakes and swamps in the southeastern U.S. Females build enormous nests of mud and leaves where they lay an average of 35 eggs. The American alligator was widely hunted for its skin in the 1900s and became endangered. Since then, it has been protected by law and its numbers have increased.

Aa

Max length 2¹/₂ feet (80 cm)
Reptile

Alligator snapping turtle

The alligator snapping turtle is the world's largest freshwater turtle, and can weigh up to 220 lbs. (100 kg) when full-grown. It has a large head with a hooked beak and very powerful jaws. The alligator snapping turtle feeds mainly on fish. It attracts its prey with a flap of skin inside its mouth that looks like a juicy, pink worm.

Aa

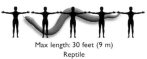

Max length: 30 feet (9 m)
Reptile

Anaconda

The anaconda is the world's heaviest snake, and can grow to up to 30 feet (9 m) in length. The anaconda is a constrictor—it uses its powerful body to prevent its prey from breathing. An adult anaconda can drag its prey underwater to drown it.

Fact

The anaconda does most of its hunting (and resting) in rivers and flooded swamps, because being in water helps support its great weight.

Max length: 7 inches (18 cm)
Amphibian

Arboreal salamander

The arboreal salamander is a small amphibian about 7 inches (18 cm) long, that is found only in the coastal forests of California. Its feet and tail are adapted for tree climbing, and it hunts among the branches for insects. It is most active during or after rain. In dry weather, it retreats to an underground burrow.

Max length: 10 inches (25 cm)
Reptile

Armadillo lizard

The armadillo lizard is a desert reptile from southern Africa. Its body is protected by strong overlapping spines and scales. When it is threatened, the armadillo lizard curls its body into a circle and holds its tail in its mouth. Its body becomes a ring of spines that protects its soft underbelly from predators.

Axolotl

Max length: 8 inches (20 cm)
Amphibian

The axolotl is a strange amphibian whose body does not change from its juvenile shape. Instead of losing its juvenile gills and developing lungs like other amphibians, the axolotl keeps its gills during adulthood and spends its whole life in water. Wild axolotls are found only in Lake Xochimilco in central Mexico. This amphibian can regrow a lost limb.

Bb

Max length: 6 inches (15 cm)
Reptile

Banded gecko

The banded gecko is a small desert lizard that spends most of the day hiding beneath rocks. It comes out at night to hunt insects and spiders. When the banded gecko is threatened by a predator, it curls its tail over its head to make itself look like a scorpion. If it is caught by its tail, the tail detaches and the gecko grows a new one.

Fact

Some geckos can climb on almost any surface—even upside down. The banded gecko is often found on the underside of rocks.

Max length: 18 inches (45 cm)
Reptile

Bearded dragon

The bearded dragon is a heavy-bodied lizard that lives in the dry forests, scrub, and semi-desert of Australia. It feeds mainly on vegetation and insects. It gets its name from its "beard," which is a jaw pouch of scales. The bearded dragon uses this "beard" to frighten predators such as snakes and birds of prey.

Black-headed python

Max length: 8 feet (2.4 m)
Reptile

The black-headed python is a slim-bodied snake that can grow to more than 8 feet (2.4 m) in length. It lives in northern Australia, where it feeds on small lizards and other snakes. The black-headed python is not venomous—it kills its victims by constriction.

Blue poison dart frog

Max length 2 inches (5 cm)
Amphibian

The blue poison dart frog does not need camouflage to keep it safe from predators in the tropical forests of Central America. The frog's skin produces chemicals that are highly poisonous, and the animal's bright coloration is a warning signal.

Bb

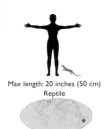

Max length: 20 inches (50 cm)
Reptile

Blue-tongued skink

The blue-tongued skink is a medium-sized reptile from eastern Australia. It eats a wide variety of food, including snails, insects, fruit, and leaves. The blue-tongued skink has no teeth to defend itself from predators. Instead, it shoots out its large, blue tongue and hisses to frighten away any attackers.

Fact
Although the blue-tongued skink has no teeth, it has powerful jaws and can give a person a painful bite.

Max length: 8 inches (20 cm)
Reptile

Broadley's flat lizard

Broadley's flat lizard is only found on rocks around waterfalls in southwestern Africa, where it feeds on fruit and insects. Sometimes, it leaps into the air to catch flies in its mouth. The lizard's unusually flat body enables it to hide from birds of prey in narrow cracks in the rocks.

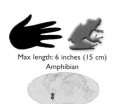

Max length: 6 inches (15 cm)
Amphibian

Budgett's frog

Budgett's frog is a strange looking amphibian from Argentina. It is camouflaged to look like a smooth river pebble. When threatened, Budgett's frog opens its huge mouth, and screams and grunts loudly. This aggressive display is enough to frighten away most predators. Those that do not run away are likely to be bitten by this fierce frog.

Max length: 8 inches (20 cm)
Amphibian

Bullfrog (North American)

The North American bullfrog is the biggest frog in North America, with a body length of up to 8 inches (20 cm). It is an aggressive predator that hunts small mammals and snakes, as well as other amphibians. The pattern on the back of the North American bullfrog varies from region to region, but in some regions it is simply green.

Cc

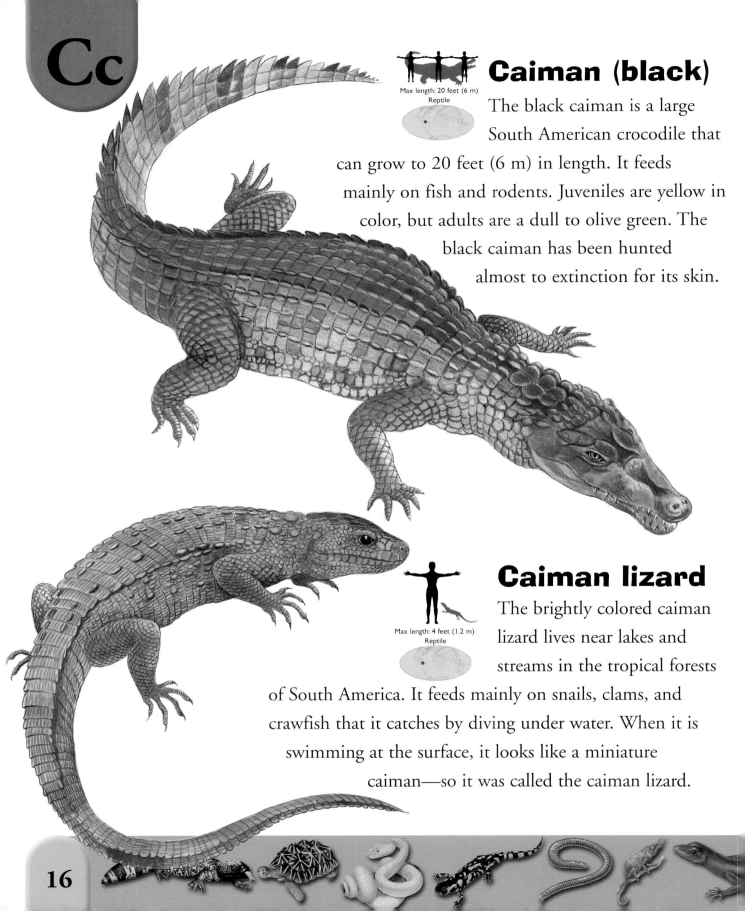

Caiman (black)

Max length: 20 feet (6 m)
Reptile

The black caiman is a large South American crocodile that can grow to 20 feet (6 m) in length. It feeds mainly on fish and rodents. Juveniles are yellow in color, but adults are a dull to olive green. The black caiman has been hunted almost to extinction for its skin.

Caiman lizard

Max length: 4 feet (1.2 m)
Reptile

The brightly colored caiman lizard lives near lakes and streams in the tropical forests of South America. It feeds mainly on snails, clams, and crawfish that it catches by diving under water. When it is swimming at the surface, it looks like a miniature caiman—so it was called the caiman lizard.

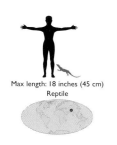

Chinese crocodile lizard

The Chinese crocodile lizard is a rare reptile from the mountain ponds and streams of southern China. It has a ridge of bony scales along its back and tail like a crocodile. If it senses danger, the Chinese crocodile lizard stops in mid-stride and remains motionless, on land or underwater, for several hours.

Max length: 18 inches (45 cm)
Reptile

Chuckwalla

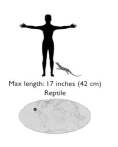

Max length: 17 inches (42 cm)
Reptile

The chuckwalla is a medium-sized desert lizard that grows to about 17 inches (42 cm) long. It feeds on cacti and other vegetation and is active only in the hottest part of the day. When threatened by a predator, the chuckwalla hides in a rock crevice and inflates its body—jammed inside the crevice, it is difficult to pull out.

Collared lizard

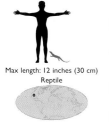

Max length: 12 inches (30 cm)
Reptile

The collared lizard is a fast moving desert predator that hunts insects and other lizards during the heat of the day. It is about 12 inches (30 cm) long when full-grown. When escaping from danger, the collared lizard lifts its front legs off the ground and runs using its powerful hind legs.

Cc

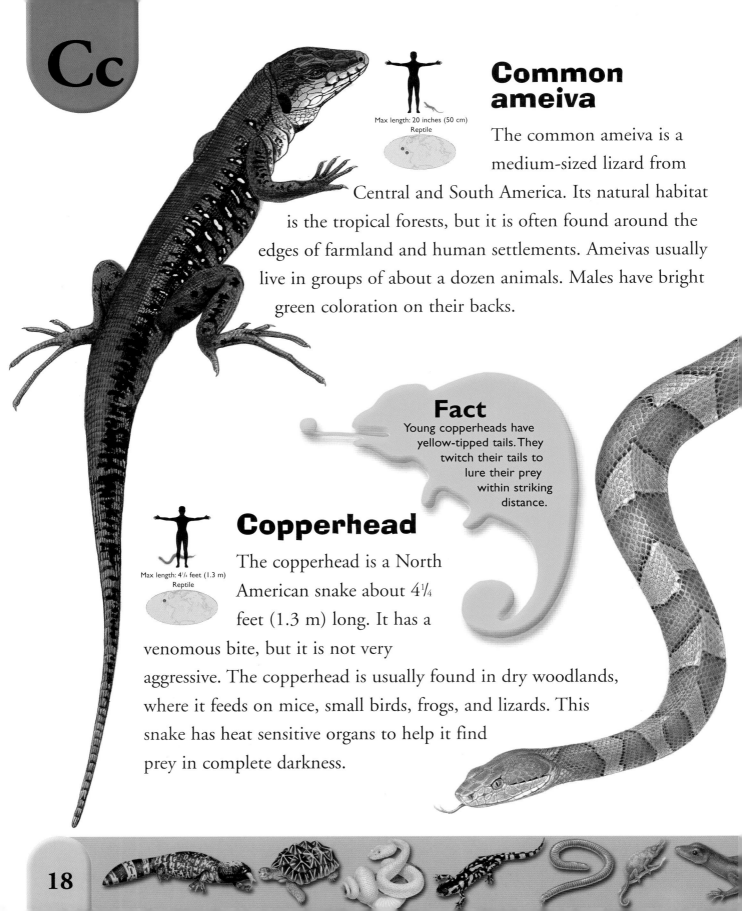

Max length: 20 inches (50 cm)
Reptile

Common ameiva

The common ameiva is a medium-sized lizard from Central and South America. Its natural habitat is the tropical forests, but it is often found around the edges of farmland and human settlements. Ameivas usually live in groups of about a dozen animals. Males have bright green coloration on their backs.

Fact
Young copperheads have yellow-tipped tails. They twitch their tails to lure their prey within striking distance.

Max length: 4¼ feet (1.3 m)
Reptile

Copperhead

The copperhead is a North American snake about 4¼ feet (1.3 m) long. It has a venomous bite, but it is not very aggressive. The copperhead is usually found in dry woodlands, where it feeds on mice, small birds, frogs, and lizards. This snake has heat sensitive organs to help it find prey in complete darkness.

Cottonmouth

Max length: 4 feet (1.2 m)
Reptile

The cottonmouth is a highly dangerous North American snake that can deliver deadly venom with its sharp fangs. It spends most of its time in or near water, and grows to about 4 feet (1.2 m) in length. The cottonmouth often becomes aggressive if disturbed—it will bite without warning. It threatens its enemies by opening its mouth to reveal the white lining.

Crocodile skink

Max length: 8 inches (20 cm)
Reptile

The crocodile skink is a small, secretive lizard from the tropical forests of New Guinea. It looks like a miniature dinosaur, with a big, triangular head and rows of spines along its back and tail. The crocodile skink spends most of its time hunting for insects and worms in the leaf litter on the forest floor.

Dd

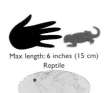

Max length: 6 inches (15 cm)
Reptile

Desert horned lizard

The desert horned lizard is a small desert
animal. It is commonly called a "horned toad"
even though it is a reptile, not an amphibian. It has a
wide, flat body with a short tail, and it feeds mainly on ants that it
gathers up with its tongue. When threatened, it squirts blood
from its eye sockets.

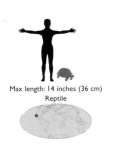

Max length: 14 inches (36 cm)
Reptile

Desert tortoise

The desert tortoise is found in the
southwestern United States and
northern Mexico. This reptile
shelters from hot and cold extremes
by digging deep burrows that can be 33 feet (10 m) long.
These burrows also provide shelter for other creatures. The desert
tortoise feeds on cacti, herbs, grasses, and some shrubs.

Fact
During the mating season,
desert tortoises can be very
aggressive and males will
attack each other
on sight.

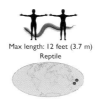

Max length: 12 feet (3.7 m)
Reptile

Diamond python

The diamond python lives in tropical forests and grassland in Australia and New Guinea. This non-venomous snake reaches a maximum length of about 12 feet (3.7 m) when full-grown. The diamond python feeds on small mammals and birds. It suffocates its victims inside its muscular coils before swallowing them whole.

Max length: 6¼ feet (1.9 m)
Reptile

Dwarf crocodile

The dwarf crocodile is found in swampy regions of tropical rainforest in central Africa. Although it is small compared to the Nile crocodile, it is a large reptile. When the forest is flooded, it eats fish, and when the water levels are lower, it feeds on crustaceans and frogs.

Ee

Max length: 3½ feet (1.8 m)
Reptile

Eastern glass lizard

The eastern glass lizard looks like a snake, but it is, in fact, a legless lizard with a long tail. It is found in the southeastern United States, and it grows to about 3½ feet (1.8 m) long. It gets its name because when it is attacked by a predator, its long tail detaches from its body—breaking like glass.

Max length: 4½ inches (11.5 cm)
Amphibian

Eastern newt

The eastern newt is also known as the red-spotted newt. This small amphibian is widespread in eastern North America. Its tadpoles do not develop directly into adults, but go through a land-living juvenile stage, when they are known as red efts. It can take up to four years for a red eft to develop into an adult eastern newt.

Max length: 10 inches (25 cm)
Reptile

Emerald tree skink

The emerald tree skink is found in New Guinea and on many other islands in the Pacific Ocean. This small reptile hunts for insects high in the branches of tropical forests. Like many other lizards, its tail can detach and wiggle to distract an attacker, while the lizard makes its escape.

European fire salamander

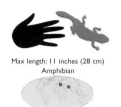

Max length: 11 inches (28 cm)
Amphibian

The European fire salamander lives in damp, hillside forests, and during the day it is most often found in the rotting interiors of fallen trees. At night, it comes out to feed on insects, slugs, and worms. Its bright coloration warns predators that this amphibian is poisonous to eat. Special glands on the salamander's head produce toxic chemicals, and it can spray them several feet.

Eyelash pit viper

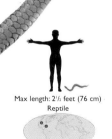

Max length: 2½ feet (76 cm)
Reptile

The eyelash pit viper is a tree-dwelling snake from the tropical forests of Central America. It gets its name from a ridge of raised scales above each eye that look like eyelashes. It grows to about 2½ feet (76 cm) and feeds on small mammals, amphibians, and lizards. The eyelash pit viper can strike fast enough to grab a hummingbird in mid-air.

Ff

Max length: 2 inches (5 cm)
Amphibian

Fire-bellied toad

The oriental fire-bellied toad, like the European fire salamander, gets its name from its bright coloration. When threatened, the toad throws itself on its back, revealing the bright colors of its underside. These colors warn predators that this toad is poisonous—it releases toxic substances through its skin.

Fact
The Florida worm lizard burrows into soft ground by using its wedge-shaped head as a battering ram.

Max length: 14 inches (36 cm)
Reptile

Florida worm lizard

The Florida worm lizard is related to the ajolote of Mexico but, like most worm lizards, it has no legs at all. The scales of this unusual reptile are arranged in rings around its body, so it looks like an earthworm. The Florida worm lizard grows to about 14 inches (36 cm) long, and spends most of its life underground, feeding on invertebrates.

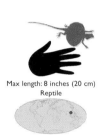

Max length: 8 inches (20 cm)
Reptile

Flying lizard

The flying lizard is a common sight on some islands in Southeast Asia. It can glide between forest trees on "wings" that extend from the sides of its body. These wings are made from skin stretched over elongated ribs. They are folded against the body while the flying lizard is hunting for ants among the branches.

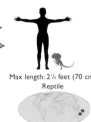

Max length: 2¼ feet (70 cm)
Reptile

Frilled lizard

The frilled lizard of Australia and New Guinea has one of the most spectacular defenses of any animal on Earth. This medium-sized reptile has a frill of skin that normally hangs around the animal's neck and shoulders. When threatened by a bird of prey, the lizard raises its frill, which makes its head look about five times bigger. The frilled lizard adds to the effect by opening its mouth wide and hissing.

Gg

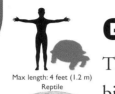

Max length: 4 feet (1.2 m)
Reptile

Galápagos tortoise

The Galápagos tortoise is the biggest tortoise in the world, weighing up to 770 lbs. (350 kg). It is only found on the remote Galápagos Islands. This tortoise can go without food and water for up to a year because it stores energy for long periods.

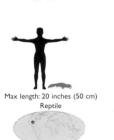

Max length: 20 inches (50 cm)
Reptile

Gila monster

The gila monster is one of only two lizards in the world that has a venomous bite (the other is the Mexican beaded lizard). It is a desert reptile and it feeds mostly on small mammals and bird eggs. It can go a long time between meals because it stores fat in its tail and abdomen. It moves slowly, but has a very powerful bite.

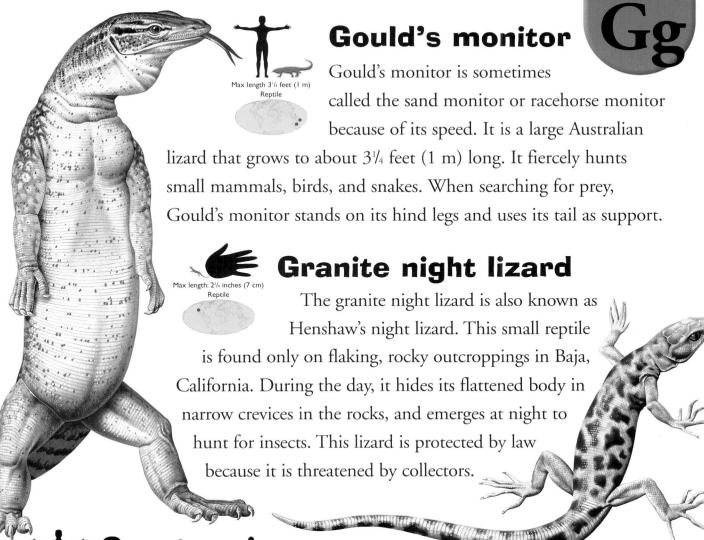

Gould's monitor

Max length 3¼ feet (1 m)
Reptile

Gould's monitor is sometimes called the sand monitor or racehorse monitor because of its speed. It is a large Australian lizard that grows to about 3¼ feet (1 m) long. It fiercely hunts small mammals, birds, and snakes. When searching for prey, Gould's monitor stands on its hind legs and uses its tail as support.

Granite night lizard

Max length: 2¾ inches (7 cm)
Reptile

The granite night lizard is also known as Henshaw's night lizard. This small reptile is found only on flaking, rocky outcroppings in Baja, California. During the day, it hides its flattened body in narrow crevices in the rocks, and emerges at night to hunt for insects. This lizard is protected by law because it is threatened by collectors.

Greater siren

Max length: 3 feet (90 cm)
Amphibian

The greater siren is a large amphibian that can reach 3 feet (90 cm) in length. It is found in shallow, muddy waters in the eastern United States. The greater siren uses gills on the outside of its head for breathing throughout its life. It has only one pair of legs at the front of its body. During dry periods, it burrows into mud where it can remain for up to two years.

Gg

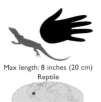

Max length: 8 inches (20 cm)
Reptile

Green anole

The green anole is a small North American lizard that is sometimes mistakenly called a chameleon. It lives in warm forests where it hunts insects among the tree branches. A male green anole has a brightly colored pouch under its throat. It can inflate this pouch as a signal to others of its kind.

Max length: 6 inches (15 cm)
Reptile

Green-blooded skink

The green-blooded skink is a small tree-dwelling reptile from the remote mountain forests of New Guinea. There are five species of green-blooded skink. These five lizards are the only land animals—out of more than 24,000 mammals, birds, reptiles, and amphibians— that have green blood. They are entirely green: they have green tongues, green bones, and even green egg shells.

Fact

Scientists believe that the color of the green-blooded skink comes from the chemicals that make it taste bitter when eaten.

Hawksbill turtle

Max length: 3 feet (90 cm)
Reptile

The hawksbill turtle is a small sea turtle that grows to no more than about 3 feet (90 cm) long. It lives in the warmer parts of the oceans, especially around coral reefs, where it feeds on sponges and shellfish. The hawksbill turtle has been hunted almost to extinction for its beautifully patterned carapace (shell).

Hellbender

Max length: 2½ feet (74 cm)
Amphibian

The hellbender is a large salamander with wrinkled skin. It is found in mountain streams in eastern North America, and it is sometimes called the "Allegheny alligator." The hellbender feeds on invertebrates that it digs up from the stream bed. Despite its scary name, this amphibian is harmless.

Hh

Max length: 16 inches (40 cm)
Reptile

Helmeted iguana

The helmeted iguana is a medium-sized reptile from the tropical forests of Central America. It gets its name from the narrow "helmet" on the back of its head. The helmeted iguana can change its color to match its surroundings. This iguana is sometimes called a basilisk.

Max length: 20 inches (50 cm)
Reptile

Horned adder

The horned adder is a small, venomous snake found in the deserts of southern Africa. When full-grown, it measures about 20 inches (50 cm). The horned adder has rough scales that help it burrow into loose sand during the day to escape the desert sun. It emerges in the evening to hunt lizards and small mammals.

Ibiza wall lizard

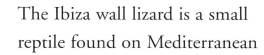

Max length: 8½ inches (21 cm)
Reptile

The Ibiza wall lizard is a small reptile found on Mediterranean islands near the coast of Spain. Its long toes help it climb quickly over walls and rocks in search of insect prey. Ibiza wall lizards gather to sun themselves on sheltered slopes in groups of up to 50 individuals.

Indian cobra

Max length: 7 feet (2.1 m)
Reptile

The Indian cobra is also known as the spectacled cobra. This large, venomous snake has markings on the back of its "hood" that look like eyes. It feeds mainly on small mammals and birds. It is extremely dangerous and kills hundreds of people each year. Indian cobras live in the grass and farmlands of India and Pakistan.

Indian starred tortoise

Max length: 11 inches (28 cm)
Reptile

The Indian starred tortoise is a medium-sized reptile that lives in scrub jungles and other dry areas. Its name comes from the star pattern on its shell. Each of the inner plates rises to a tall, rounded point. These points make the carapace much stronger, and far more difficult for a predator to crush.

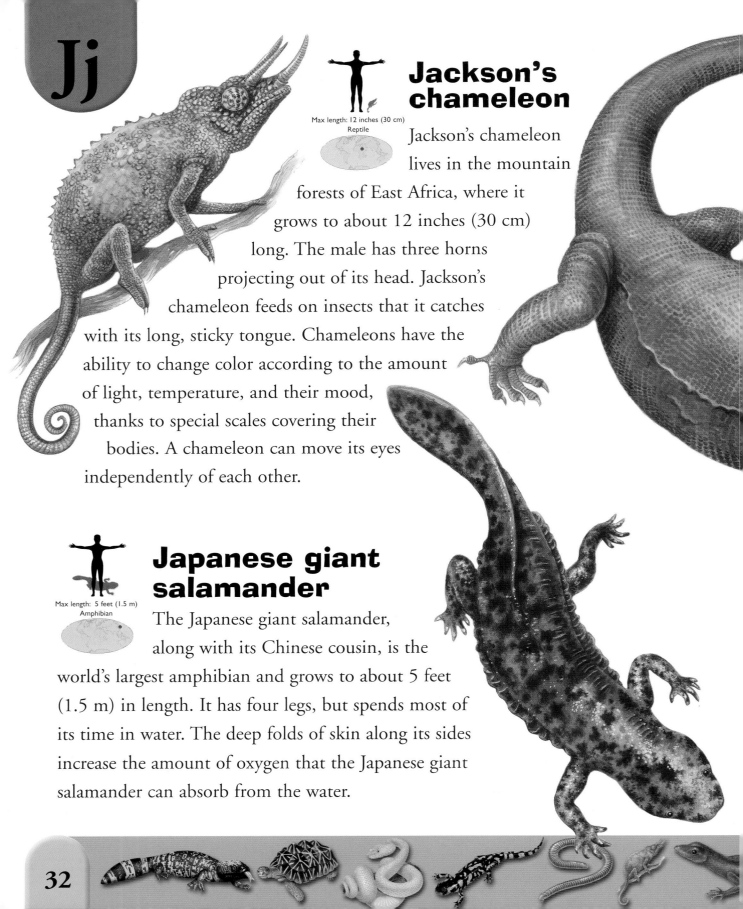

Jj

Jackson's chameleon

Max length: 12 inches (30 cm)
Reptile

Jackson's chameleon lives in the mountain forests of East Africa, where it grows to about 12 inches (30 cm) long. The male has three horns projecting out of its head. Jackson's chameleon feeds on insects that it catches with its long, sticky tongue. Chameleons have the ability to change color according to the amount of light, temperature, and their mood, thanks to special scales covering their bodies. A chameleon can move its eyes independently of each other.

Japanese giant salamander

Max length: 5 feet (1.5 m)
Amphibian

The Japanese giant salamander, along with its Chinese cousin, is the world's largest amphibian and grows to about 5 feet (1.5 m) in length. It has four legs, but spends most of its time in water. The deep folds of skin along its sides increase the amount of oxygen that the Japanese giant salamander can absorb from the water.

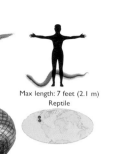

Max length: 7 feet (2.1 m)
Reptile

Kingsnake

The common kingsnake is a medium-sized snake that can reach 7 feet (2.1 m) in length. There are a number of subspecies, each with its own pattern and coloration. The common kingsnake is an aggressive predator that kills its prey by constriction. It feeds on small mammals, birds, and other reptiles—it will even attack venomous snakes because other snakes' venom has no effect on the kingsnake.

Max length: 10 feet (3 m)
Reptile

Komodo dragon

The Komodo dragon is the world's biggest lizard. A male can weigh more than 220 lbs. (100 kg). With powerful jaws and sharp claws, the Komodo dragon is a fierce hunter and has been known to bring down deer and even water buffalo. It can run at speeds up to 11 mph (18 km/h) for short periods of time.

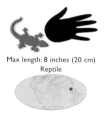

Max length: 8 inches (20 cm)
Reptile

Kuhl's flying gecko

Kuhl's flying gecko is a small lizard from the forests of Southeast Asia. It is well camouflaged for life in the trees, and spends most of its time hunting for insects. When threatened, it can glide from branch to branch thanks to its webbed feet and flaps of skin along its body and back legs. Kuhl's flying gecko uses its wave-edged tail to control the direction of its glide.

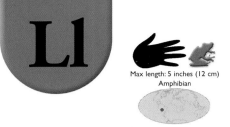

Ll

Lake Titicaca frog

Max length: 5 inches (12 cm)
Amphibian

The Lake Titicaca frog is the world's highest-living amphibian. It is found only around Lake Titicaca, which is some 12,500 feet (3,800 m) above sea level. At this height, both air and water are low in oxygen. As well as having a pair of lungs, the Lake Titicaca frog absorbs oxygen over the entire surface of its skin.

Leopard frog

Max length: 5 inches (12 cm)
Amphibian

The North American leopard frog is either green or brown in color, with rows of irregular, dark spots. This small amphibian can reach about 5 inches (12 cm). It is often seen during the summer near ponds and streams. In the winter, the leopard frog remains hidden beneath rocks or fallen trees.

Leopard tortoise

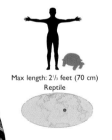

Max length: 2¹/₃ feet (70 cm)
Reptile

The leopard tortoise is a medium-sized reptile that can reach just over 2 feet (60 cm) in length. It has a domed yellow carapace (shell) with dark markings. In some individuals, these markings look like a leopard's spots. The leopard tortoise feeds on low-growing plants and fallen fruit.

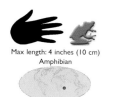

Max length: 4 inches (10 cm)
Amphibian

Madagascan tomato frog

The Madagascan tomato frog is a small, brightly colored amphibian whose females can measure 4 inches (10 cm) long. It is found only in the remote northwestern corner of Madagascar, and was once seriously endangered by forest clearance. Tomato frogs hunt for food by sitting in one spot and waiting for an insect to walk by.

Mm

Fact
The black mamba is not actually black—it is either brown or gray. Its relative the green mamba really is green.

Max length: 11 feet (3.4 m)
Reptile

Mamba (black)

The black mamba is the world's fastest-moving snake. It can race across the ground at speeds up to 12 mph (19 km/h). It is an excellent tree-climber, and may strike at its victims from the branches. It is an extremely dangerous snake because of its deadly venom and speed. The black mamba gets its name because the inside of its mouth is black.

Mm

Max length: 7 inches (18 cm)
Amphibian

Mandarin salamander

The mandarin salamander is also known as the crocodile salamander. Its distinctive black and orange markings make it look like a crocodile. This small amphibian is found mainly in damp woodland, where it burrows into the ground in search of earthworms and other soft-bodied prey.

Fact
The mandarin salamander approaches prey very slowly. Then it grabs its victim with a quick sideways movement of its head.

Max length: 6½ inches (16 cm)
Amphibian

Marbled newt

The marbled newt is found in lakes, ponds, and slow-moving rivers in southwestern Europe. This amphibian can reach 6½ inches (16 cm) in length, and has a distinctive crest along its back and tail. It has a black and green marbled coloring.

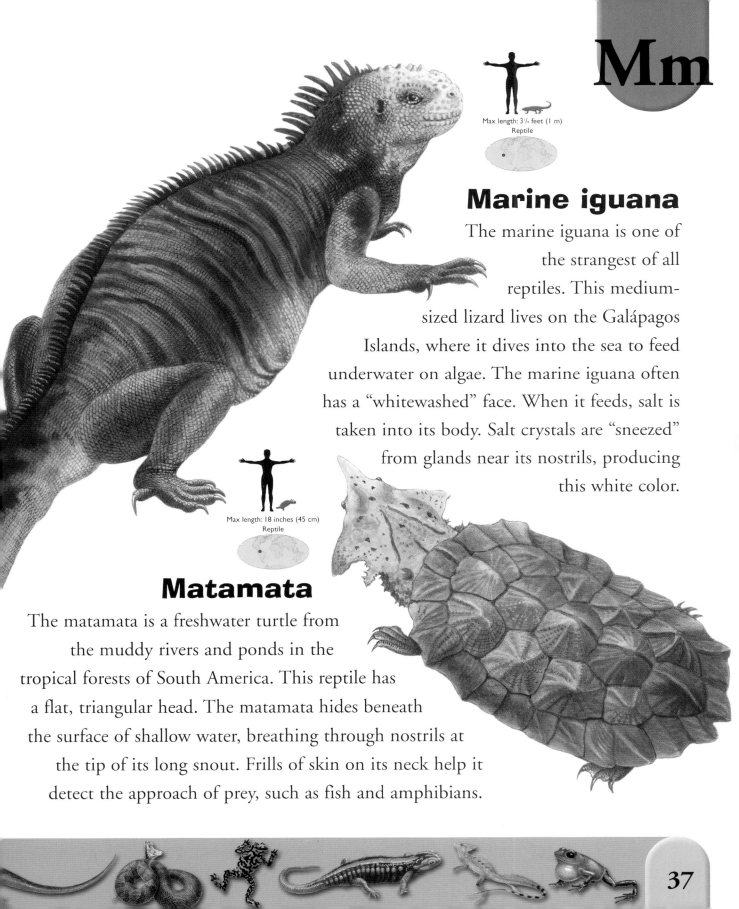

Max length: 3¼ feet (1 m)
Reptile

Marine iguana

The marine iguana is one of the strangest of all reptiles. This medium-sized lizard lives on the Galápagos Islands, where it dives into the sea to feed underwater on algae. The marine iguana often has a "whitewashed" face. When it feeds, salt is taken into its body. Salt crystals are "sneezed" from glands near its nostrils, producing this white color.

Max length: 18 inches (45 cm)
Reptile

Matamata

The matamata is a freshwater turtle from the muddy rivers and ponds in the tropical forests of South America. This reptile has a flat, triangular head. The matamata hides beneath the surface of shallow water, breathing through nostrils at the tip of its long snout. Frills of skin on its neck help it detect the approach of prey, such as fish and amphibians.

Mm

Max length: 3¼ feet (1 m)
Reptile

Mexican beaded lizard

The Mexican beaded lizard is one of only two venomous lizards— the other is the gila monster. Both species are found in the deserts of southwestern North America. The Mexican beaded lizard has the same rounded scales as the gila monster, but has a duller color. It has powerful front legs for burrowing beneath the desert surface.

Max length: 19½ inches (49 cm)
Amphibian

Mudpuppy

The mudpuppy is widespread across North America and grows up to 19½ inches (49 cm) long. Like the greater siren, it lives in water for most of its life and breathes through large, feathery gills on the sides of its head. The mudpuppy is very sensitive to water quality, and it has disappeared from many polluted rivers.

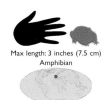

Max length: 3 inches (7.5 cm)
Amphibian

Natterjack toad

The natterjack toad is a small European amphibian that grows to about 3 inches (7.5 cm) long. It has a dark coloring with a yellow stripe along the center of its back. The natterjack toad prefers open landscapes with sandy soil, and is sometimes found near coastal sand dunes. The natterjack tends to run instead of hopping like other toads.

Max length: 20 feet (6 m)
Reptile

Nile crocodile

The Nile crocodile is a very dangerous reptile that can grow to 20 feet (6 m) in length. It feeds by ambushing prey at the edges of rivers and lakes. The Nile crocodile attacks and eats prey as large as a zebra or water buffalo. It drags its victim underwater to drown it.

Max length: 8½ inches (21 cm)
Reptile

Northern leaf-tailed gecko

The northern leaf-tailed gecko is a small reptile that lives in the tropical forests of northern and eastern Australia. Its body is flat so it does not make a shadow, and is camouflaged to look like the bark of a tree. This "woody" appearance continues along its tail that is shaped like a leaf, which can be dropped and regrown.

Oo

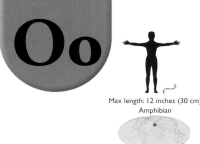

Max length: 12 inches (30 cm)
Amphibian

Olm

The olm is a strange salamander that is only found in some caves in southern Europe. This amphibian has become adapted to life in complete darkness. Its skin has almost no coloration, and it has nearly lost the use of its eyes. The olm uses its sense of smell to hunt for small invertebrates in underground streams.

Ornate horned toad

Max length: 8 inches (20 cm)
Amphibian

The ornate horned toad is a fat-bodied amphibian that grows to about 8 inches (20 cm) in length. It spends most of its time on the ground, half-buried among fallen leaves and moss, waiting for prey to approach. When a mouse or small lizard comes too close, the toad opens its wide mouth, full of large, sharp teeth, and swallows its prey in one gulp.

Fact
The ornate patterns that give this toad its name are a highly effective form of camouflage.

Pacific giant salamander

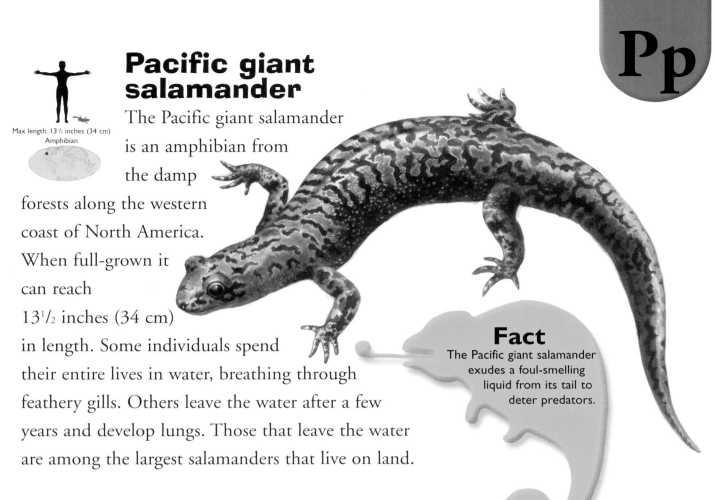

Max length: 13½ inches (34 cm)
Amphibian

The Pacific giant salamander is an amphibian from the damp forests along the western coast of North America. When full-grown it can reach 13½ inches (34 cm) in length. Some individuals spend their entire lives in water, breathing through feathery gills. Others leave the water after a few years and develop lungs. Those that leave the water are among the largest salamanders that live on land.

Fact
The Pacific giant salamander exudes a foul-smelling liquid from its tail to deter predators.

Pacific ground boa

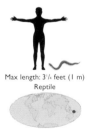

Max length: 3¼ feet (1 m)
Reptile

The Pacific ground boa from New Guinea has two subspecies. One is fat-bodied and hunts prey on the ground. The other subspecies has a narrower body and spends most of its time in the trees. The Pacific ground boa is non-venomous and kills its prey by constriction.

Pp

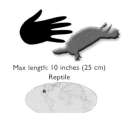

Max length: 10 inches (25 cm)
Reptile

Painted turtle

The painted turtle is widespread in North America, where it grows to about 10 inches (25 cm) long. It is often seen on rocks and logs in the mornings, warming itself in sunlight. When threatened by a predator, such as a raccoon, the painted turtle pulls its head back into its carapace.

Fact
Young painted turtles are meat eaters, but as they grow up, they become vegetarian, or plant eaters.

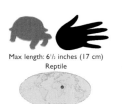

Max length: 6½ inches (17 cm)
Reptile

Pancake tortoise

The pancake tortoise is a small African reptile about 6½ inches (17 cm) long. It has a very flat carapace (shell) with plates that are flexible, not fixed in a rigid shape. This flexible shell allows the pancake tortoise to squeeze itself beneath rocks to hide from birds of prey and other predators.

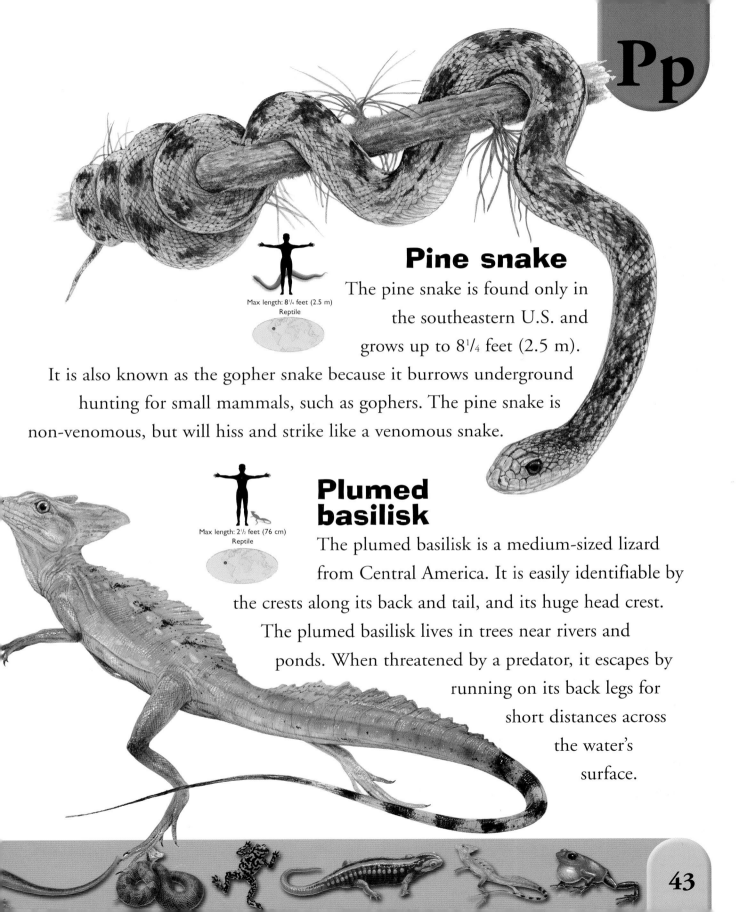

Pine snake

Max length: 8¼ feet (2.5 m)
Reptile

The pine snake is found only in the southeastern U.S. and grows up to 8¼ feet (2.5 m). It is also known as the gopher snake because it burrows underground hunting for small mammals, such as gophers. The pine snake is non-venomous, but will hiss and strike like a venomous snake.

Plumed basilisk

Max length: 2½ feet (76 cm)
Reptile

The plumed basilisk is a medium-sized lizard from Central America. It is easily identifiable by the crests along its back and tail, and its huge head crest. The plumed basilisk lives in trees near rivers and ponds. When threatened by a predator, it escapes by running on its back legs for short distances across the water's surface.

Qq Rr

Queensland cane toad

Max length: 9 inches (23 cm)
Amphibian

The Queensland cane toad is also known as the marine toad. This aggressive amphibian lives in the tropical forests of South and Central America. It was introduced to Queensland, Australia, to combat insect pests that were attacking the sugar cane crop. A cane toad will eat almost anything it can swallow.

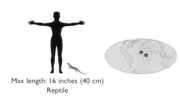

Max length: 16 inches (40 cm)
Reptile

Rainbow lizard

The rainbow lizard is a medium-sized reptile that is widespread across central Africa. When full-grown, it measures about 16 inches (40 cm) long. Only males have the bright red and blue coloration that give this lizard its name—females and juveniles are dull gray. At night, the males turn gray, but when their bodies warm up in the morning sunlight, they become colored again.

Fact

Male rainbow lizards fight each other using sideways blows of their tails. The defeated male turns a dull gray color.

Red-eared slider turtle

Max length: 12 inches (30 cm)
Reptile

The red-eared slider turtle is widespread in the lakes, rivers, and streams of the central United States. It grows to about 12 inches (30 cm) in length. Its red "ears" are, in fact, a pair of distinctive red stripes, one behind each eye. The red-eared turtle likes to bask in warm sunlight. Sometimes these turtles "stack up" on top of each other in their efforts to get the best basking position.

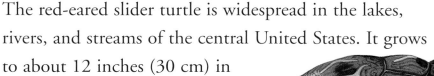

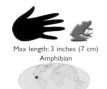

Max length: 3 inches (7 cm)
Amphibian

Red-eyed tree frog

The red-eyed tree frog is a small amphibian from South and Central America that spends most of its life in the trees. In the breeding season, it lays eggs on leaves above small ponds, and when the tadpoles hatch, they drop into the water. It has brightly colored markings on its sides, which can be covered by its green legs for good camouflage.

Max length: 4 feet (1.2 m)
Reptile

Red spitting cobra

The red spitting cobra is a venomous snake from eastern Africa that measures up to 4 feet (1.2 m). It has a very special method of attacking its prey. It does not bite its victims to inject its venom. Instead, it sprays a cloud of venomous droplets up to 6 feet (1.8 m) into its prey's eyes. The venom causes instant blindness and makes the prey helpless.

Max length: 4 inches (10 cm)
Amphibian

Reinwardt's flying frog

Reinwardt's flying frog is found in the tropical forests of Indonesia. Like some of its close relatives, it has developed the ability to "fly," or "glide" between tree branches. Reinwardt's flying frog has large back feet with wide webs of skin between the toes. These webs act like parachutes as the frog glides through the air.

Ringed caecilian

The ringed caecilian is also known as the South American caecilian. It belongs to a group of amphibians—the caecilians—that are rarely seen because they live underground, and sometimes under the mud at the bottom of lakes. The ringed caecilian has distinctive pale rings around its wormlike body. Caecilians may look like worms, but they have sharp, needle-like teeth.

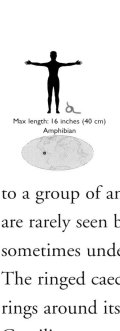

Max length: 16 inches (40 cm)
Amphibian

Max length: 5 feet (1.5 m)
Reptile

Round Island keel-scaled boa

The Round Island keel-scaled boa is one of the world's rarest snakes, because it is found only on a single small island in the Indian Ocean. It gets part of its name from the shape of its scales, each of which has a central ridge known as a keel. Unlike most boas, which give birth to live young, the Round Island keel-scaled boa lays eggs.

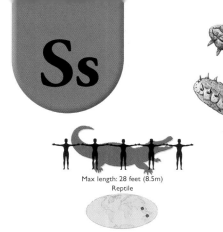

Max length: 28 feet (8.5m)
Reptile

Saltwater crocodile

The saltwater crocodile is the largest and most
dangerous reptile in the world. It is found in bays
and estuaries around the coastline of the southern
Pacific and Indian oceans. A full-grown saltwater crocodile
can measure more than 28 feet (8.5 m) in length, and will
eat almost anything it can overpower, including humans.

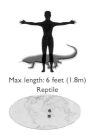

Max length: 6 feet (1.8m)
Reptile

Savanna monitor

The Savanna monitor is a large lizard from the grasslands of
Africa that can reach about 6 feet (1.8 m) in length. It is also
known as the white-throated monitor. When threatened, the
savanna monitor puffs up its
pale-colored throat and
body to make it look
even bigger and
more fierce.
Then it whips its tail
from side to side.

Serrated hinge-back tortoise

Max length: 12½ inches (32 cm)
Reptile

The serrated hinge-back tortoise is found in central Africa and prefers a forest habitat. This medium-sized reptile grows to just over 12½ inches (32 cm) in length. It gets its name from the design of its carapace (shell), which can be folded down to completely protect the animal inside. The sharp serrations around the edge of the carapace also help to deter predators.

Sidewinder

Max length: 2 feet (60 cm)
Reptile

The sidewinder is a large, venomous snake from the deserts of southwestern North America. Instead of slithering forward head first like most snakes, the sidewinder moves across the ground in a series of sideways S-shapes. This method of movement means that only a small area of the snake's body is in contact with the hot desert surface.

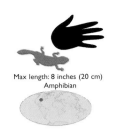

Max length: 8 inches (20 cm)
Amphibian

Slimy salamander

The slimy salamander is widespread in the eastern U.S. This amphibian grows to about 8 inches (20 cm) in length.

The slimy salamander has a dark-colored body with white or silver spots, and it is only seen at night. As a defense, its skin produces a very sticky slime, which makes this animal an unpleasant mouthful for a predator.

Fact

One difference between slow worms and snakes is that a slow worm has movable eyelids and a snake does not.

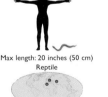

Max length: 20 inches (50 cm)
Reptile

Slow worm

The slow worm is a legless lizard that is often mistaken for a snake. It measures about 20 inches (50 cm) long, and it is widespread across Europe. The slow worm spends most of its time under logs, stones, and deep undergrowth hunting for slugs and insects. Like some other lizards, it sheds its tail to escape from predators.

Snake-necked turtle

The snake-necked turtle is found in the rivers of eastern Australia. The head and neck of this unusual reptile are often longer than the rest of its body. The snake-necked turtle shoots out its long neck to snatch passing fish. The long neck also allows the turtle to breathe at the surface while its body remains completely under water.

Max length: 10 inches (25 cm)
Reptile

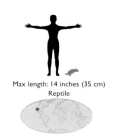

Max length: 14 inches (35 cm)
Reptile

Softshell turtle

The smooth softshell turtle is found in central parts of the U.S. Unlike other turtles, it does not have a bony carapace (shell). Instead, its shell is covered with leathery skin. The smooth softshell turtle often makes its nest on sandbars in the middle of slow-moving rivers. Females reach about 14 inches (35 cm) in length, but males are only half this size.

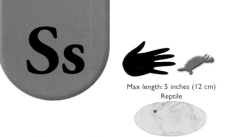

Ss

Max length: 5 inches (12 cm)
Reptile

Stinkpot

The stinkpot is a small turtle from the southeastern U.S. about 5 inches (12 cm) long. Although it is small in size, it packs a very powerful and unpleasant surprise. When disturbed, the stinkpot releases a foul-smelling substance from special glands. It can also deliver a very painful bite.

Max length: 1 inch (2.5 cm)
Amphibian

Strawberry poison dart frog

The strawberry poison dart frog is one of the most brightly colored amphibians. These tiny frogs are often spotted or striped, and they vary in color depending on their location. These bright colors are warnings to predators that the frogs' skin is poisonous.

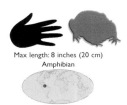

Max length: 8 inches (20 cm)
Amphibian

Surinam toad

The Surinam toad is found in South America, where it spends its entire life in water. It has a flattened body with a triangular head, and grows to about 8 inches (20 cm) in length. The Surinam toad has special sense organs along its sides to help it find food in muddy water. It also has thin tentacles on the tips of its fingers to increase its sense of touch.

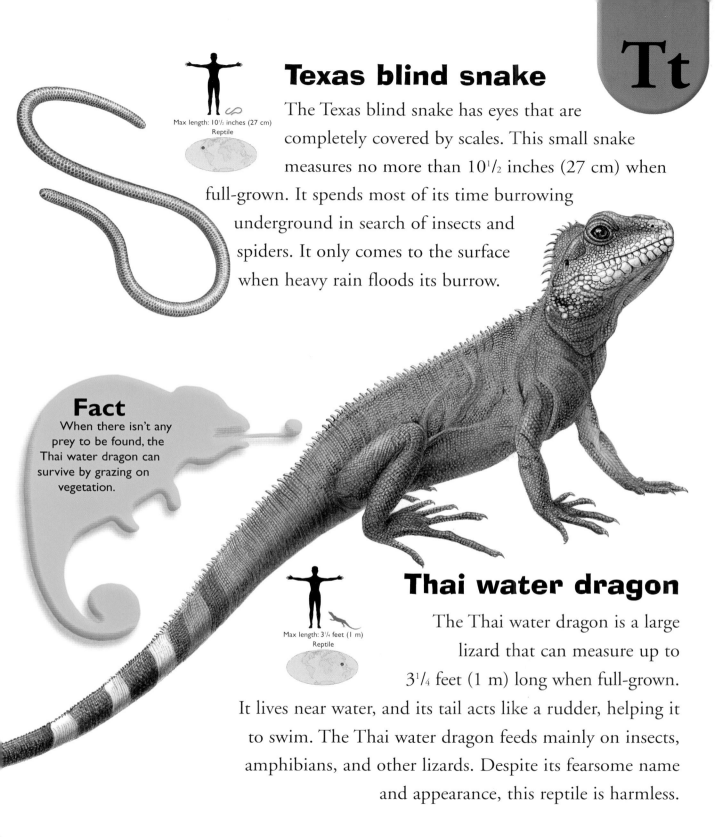

Texas blind snake

Max length: 10½ inches (27 cm)
Reptile

The Texas blind snake has eyes that are completely covered by scales. This small snake measures no more than 10½ inches (27 cm) when full-grown. It spends most of its time burrowing underground in search of insects and spiders. It only comes to the surface when heavy rain floods its burrow.

Fact

When there isn't any prey to be found, the Thai water dragon can survive by grazing on vegetation.

Thai water dragon

Max length: 3¼ feet (1 m)
Reptile

The Thai water dragon is a large lizard that can measure up to 3¼ feet (1 m) long when full-grown. It lives near water, and its tail acts like a rudder, helping it to swim. The Thai water dragon feeds mainly on insects, amphibians, and other lizards. Despite its fearsome name and appearance, this reptile is harmless.

Tt

Max length: 7 inches (18 cm)
Reptile

Thorny devil

The thorny devil is a lizard from the deserts of western Australia. This bizarre-looking reptile is only 7 inches (18 cm) long, and well camouflaged. The thorny devil moves very slowly, and cannot run away from predators. For protection, it relies on sharp spines that cover the head, body, and tail.

Max length: 14 inches (35 cm)
Amphibian

Tiger salamander

The tiger salamander is widespread in North America. There are several subspecies, some of which have yellow and black markings, while others are mostly green or brown. When full-grown, the tiger salamander measures about 14 inches (35 cm) long, and rivals the Pacific giant salamander as the largest land-living salamander.

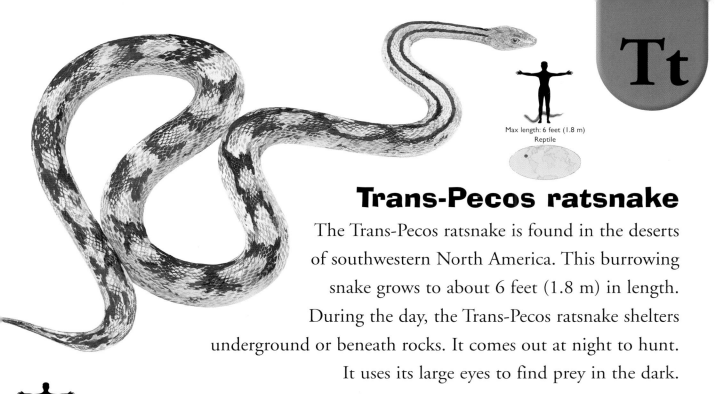

Max length: 6 feet (1.8 m)
Reptile

Trans-Pecos ratsnake

The Trans-Pecos ratsnake is found in the deserts of southwestern North America. This burrowing snake grows to about 6 feet (1.8 m) in length. During the day, the Trans-Pecos ratsnake shelters underground or beneath rocks. It comes out at night to hunt. It uses its large eyes to find prey in the dark.

Max length: 2 feet (60 cm)
Reptile

Tuatara

The tuatara is an ancient and rare creature found on islands near the coast of New Zealand. It can reach about 2 feet (60 cm) in length and feeds on insects and worms. Although it looks like an iguana, it is part of a separate group of reptiles. Its scales and bone structures are more closely related to reptiles that became extinct over 200 million years ago.

Uu
Vv

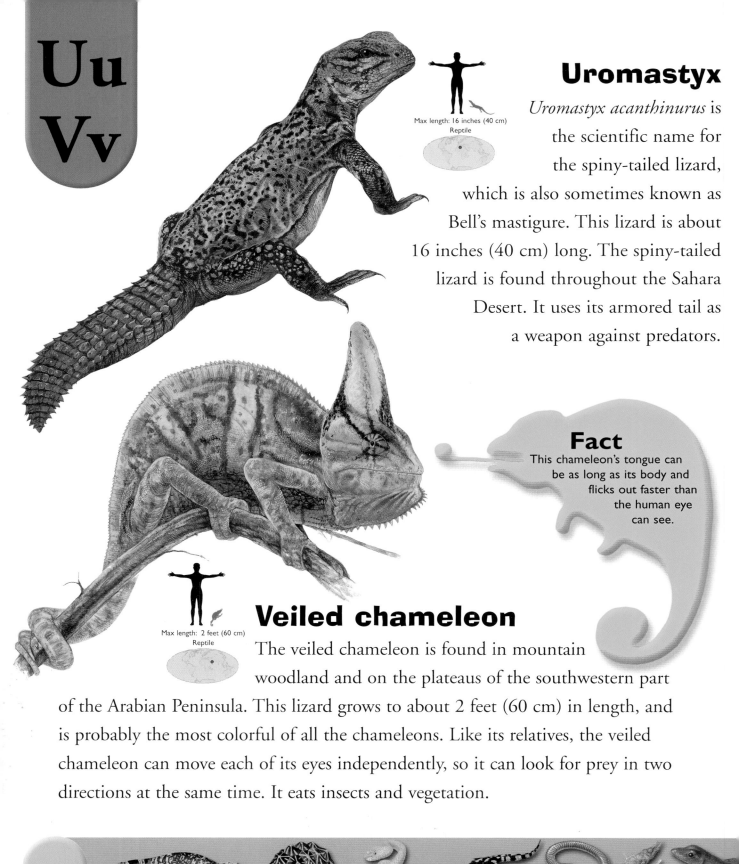

Uromastyx

Max length: 16 inches (40 cm)
Reptile

Uromastyx acanthinurus is the scientific name for the spiny-tailed lizard, which is also sometimes known as Bell's mastigure. This lizard is about 16 inches (40 cm) long. The spiny-tailed lizard is found throughout the Sahara Desert. It uses its armored tail as a weapon against predators.

Fact
This chameleon's tongue can be as long as its body and flicks out faster than the human eye can see.

Veiled chameleon

Max length: 2 feet (60 cm)
Reptile

The veiled chameleon is found in mountain woodland and on the plateaus of the southwestern part of the Arabian Peninsula. This lizard grows to about 2 feet (60 cm) in length, and is probably the most colorful of all the chameleons. Like its relatives, the veiled chameleon can move each of its eyes independently, so it can look for prey in two directions at the same time. It eats insects and vegetation.

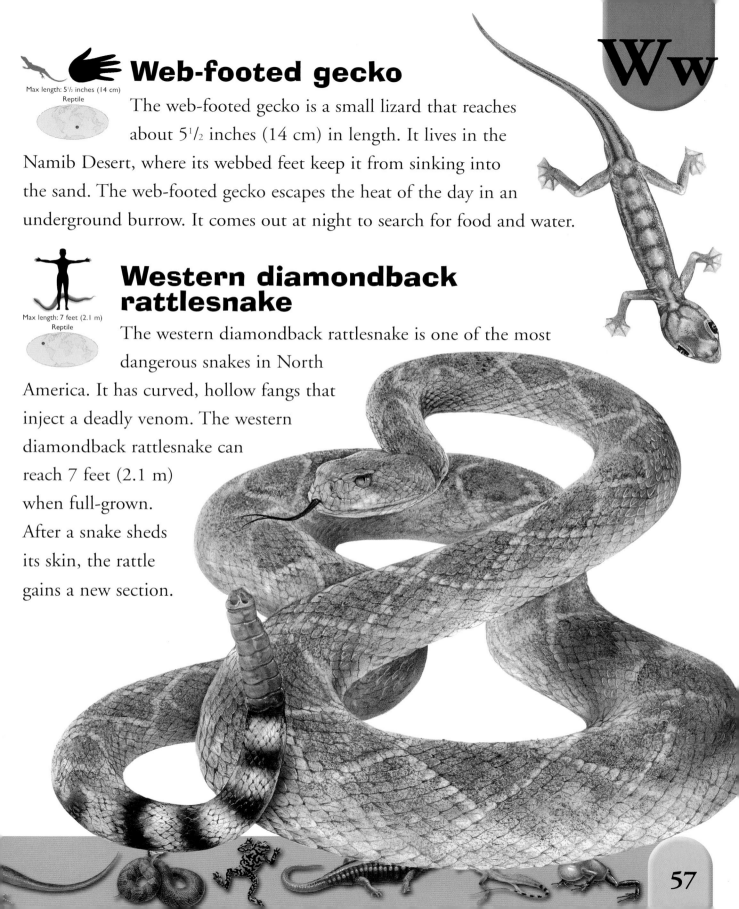

Web-footed gecko

Max length: 5½ inches (14 cm)
Reptile

The web-footed gecko is a small lizard that reaches about 5½ inches (14 cm) in length. It lives in the Namib Desert, where its webbed feet keep it from sinking into the sand. The web-footed gecko escapes the heat of the day in an underground burrow. It comes out at night to search for food and water.

Western diamondback rattlesnake

Max length: 7 feet (2.1 m)
Reptile

The western diamondback rattlesnake is one of the most dangerous snakes in North America. It has curved, hollow fangs that inject a deadly venom. The western diamondback rattlesnake can reach 7 feet (2.1 m) when full-grown. After a snake sheds its skin, the rattle gains a new section.

Ww

Ww
Xx

Wood turtle

Max length: 7¹/₂ inches (19 cm)
Reptile

The wood turtle lives along forested rivers and streams in North America. This small reptile grows to about 7¹/₂ inches (19 cm) in length. Although the wood turtle spends a lot of its time in the water, it often wanders through the woods in search of food, such as worms, insects, leaves, and berries.

Max length: 5¹/₂ inches (13 cm)
Amphibian

Xenopus laevis

Xenopus laevis is the scientific name for the African clawed frog. This amphibian is about 5¹/₂ inches (13 cm) long, and it spends most of its time at the bottom of muddy ponds and lakes. The African clawed frog has a row of special sense organs along its sides. These organs help it to detect prey, and it will eat almost anything.

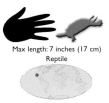

Max length: 7 inches (17 cm)
Reptile

Yellow-blotched map turtle

The yellow-blotched map turtle is also known as the yellow-blotched sawback. This reptile grows to about 7 inches (17 cm) long, and is found only in slow-moving rivers in the state of Mississippi, USA, where it feeds on insects and shellfish. The yellow-blotched map turtle is endangered by the destruction of its habitat.

Max length: 7 inches (17 cm)
Reptile

Zimbabwe girdled lizard

The Zimbabwe girdled lizard is a small reptile about 7 inches (17 cm) long. It lives in burrows beneath rocky ground. The lizard has a tail covered with backward-pointing spiny scales. These scales make its tail look like an elongated pine cone. When threatened, this lizard runs into a crack in the rocks and raises its spines so it cannot be pulled out.

Glossary

Amphibian An air-breathing, cold-blooded vertebrate that mostly lays jelly-covered eggs. Frogs, toads, newts, and salamanders are the most common amphibians.

Amphisbaenian An unusual type of burrowing reptile that is often called a worm-lizard.

Arboreal Describes an animal that climbs well and spends most of its time in trees.

Cacti A group of drought-resistant desert plants, most of which have spines instead of leaves.

Caecilian An unusual type of wormlike, burrowing amphibian.

Camouflage Shape, color, and pattern that help an animal blend in with its background, so its enemies—and its prey—cannot see it easily.

Carapace The dome-shaped "shell" of tortoises and turtles; made up of overlapping scutes that are usually fused together into a solid dome.

Cold-blooded An animal that relies on the environment to maintain its body temperature; fish, amphibians, and reptiles are the main groups of cold-blooded vertebrates.

Constriction The method by which some snakes kill their prey. The snake coils tightly around its victim to prevent it from inflating its lungs and breathing; death is caused by suffocation.

Endangered Describes a species that has such a small remaining population that it is in danger of becoming extinct.

Estuary The lowest part of a river, where it enters the ocean. The water in an estuary is a mixture of fresh water and salty ocean water.

Fang A long, sharp tooth designed for seizing prey. A number of snakes have hollow fangs that inject venom when they bite.

Freshwater The word used to describe the water from rainfall, rivers, and most lakes. It does not contain salt.

Glossary

Gills Organs that extract oxygen from the water. Before metamorphosis, amphibians breathe through gills, although most develop lungs when they become adults.

Habitat The combination of landscape, climate, vegetation, and animal life that forms the natural environment for a particular species.

Invertebrate An animal that does not have an internal skeleton with a backbone. Insects, snails, spiders, worms, and millipedes are all invertebrates.

Juvenile An animal that is not full-grown.

Lungs The breathing organs (usually a pair) used by mammals, birds, reptiles, and most amphibians.

Mammal A warm-blooded vertebrate animal that produces live-born young. Most mammals are covered with hair and live on land.

Marine Describes something that is associated with the seas and oceans.

Metamorphosis The process by which amphibians and many insects change from a juvenile body shape to an adult shape.

Oxygen The chemical gas in air, which is essential for living things. Land animals take oxygen directly from the air into their lungs. Animals with gills can extract oxygen from the surrounding water.

Polluted Describes environments and habitats that are affected by the presence of unnatural substances, such as chemicals from vehicle exhausts.

Glossary

Predator An animal that hunts and eats other animals.

Prey An animal that is hunted and eaten by others.

Reptile A cold-blooded, air-breathing, vertebrate animal that lays eggs mostly on land. Crocodiles, lizards, turtles, tortoises, and snakes are all reptiles.

Ribs Part of the vertebrate skeleton— pairs of ribs curve around the major internal organs (such as the heart and the lungs), to protect them from injury.

Scales Small, disc-like plates that protect the skin of fish and reptiles. Reptile scales can be smooth or rough, and may be triangular in cross-section.

Scutes Large, bony scales that protect the skin of alligators, crocodiles, tortoises, and turtles. The scales on a snake's head are also called scutes.

Shellfish A non-scientific term for invertebrate water creatures (such as crustaceans and most mollusks) that have a hard outer shell.

Species A particular scientific group to which an individual animal (or plant) belongs. Each species is a unique design for life and has a two-part scientific name. Members of the same species all share characteristics and differ only slightly in coloration or size.

Sub-species A group of animals belonging to the same species that share the same variation in their characteristic features. Some animals that are widely distributed have a number of regional sub-species.

Tadpole The juvenile life-stage of a frog or toad; tadpoles are legless, live entirely in water, and breathe through gills.

Temperate Regions that have warm summers and cool winters, and occur between the subtropics and the poles.

Glossary

Toxic Poisonous. A toxin is a poison produced inside the body of a living thing.

Tropical Regions around the Equator, between the Tropic of Cancer and the Tropic of Capricorn. A tropical climate is usually hot and rainy.

Venomous Capable of delivering a poisonous bite or sting; venom is any poison produced by an animal for the purpose of injuring another animal.

Vertebrate An animal that has an internal skeleton arranged around a backbone; fish, amphibians, reptiles, birds, and mammals are all vertebrates.

Warm-blooded
An animal that uses some of the energy it gets from food to maintain its body temperature at a constant level. Mammals and birds are warm-blooded.

Webbed Describes a hand or foot in which the individual fingers or toes are joined together by flaps of skin.

Index